ISABELLA GARDNER:

the collected poems

ISABELLA GARDNER:

the collected poems

BOA EDITIONS, LTD. • BROCKPORT • NY • 1990

ISBN: 0-918526-72-8 Cloth
ISBN: 0-918526-73-6 Paper

LC #: 89-62536
First Edition

Publications by BOA Editions, Ltd., a small, non-profit and tax-exempt literary organiza-
tion, are made possible with the assistance of grants from the Literature Program of the
New York State Council on the Arts and the Literature Program of the National Endow-
ment for the Arts, as well as grants and donations from private individuals, corporations
and foundations.

The publishers are grateful to the family of Isabella Gardner for their encouragement and
cooperation during the preparation of *Isabella Gardner: The Collected Poems*.

Cover Photograph: "Calla Lily 1987"
Copyright 1987 by The Estate of Robert Mapplethorpe

Photograph of Isabella Gardner:
Copyright 1981 by Layle Silbert

Cover Design:
Daphne Poulin

BOA Logo:
Mirko

BOA Editions, Ltd.
A. Poulin, Jr., President
92 Park Avenue
Brockport, NY 14420

CONTENTS

(Poems that Isabella Gardner included in more than one collection appear under the title of the book in which they were first collected.)

The Looking Glass (1961)

West of Childhood (1965)

That Was Then: New and Selected Poems (1980)

I. THE ACCOMPLICES

II. PART OF THE DARKNESS

ISABELLA GARDNER:

the collected poems

Birthdays from the Ocean
(1955)

THAT "CRANING OF THE NECK"

> *The primary word is I-Thou. The primary word*
> *I-Thou can only be spoken with the whole*
> *being. The primary word I-It can never be*
> *spoken with the whole being.*
> — Martin Buber

Birthdays from the ocean one desert april noon
I rode through the untouching and no-odored air
astride an english saddle on a western mare
through the resisting tow-colored grass and the dune-
less sand. Under me swam a stream strange in that dried
country. A "great blue heron" stood still in the tide-
less water and when I saw him there my heart daz-
zled. I whispered the mare to move quietly as
Indians move, I reined her with a catpaw hand
and my breathless feet crouched into the stirrups and
I prayed her through cactus mesquite and cattlebones
to the water's edge where the tall bird fished the stones.
The listening heron expanded with despair
unloosed unwilling wings, heaved from water into air.
O he hated to fly he flapped with a splayed pain-
ful motion. Deliberate as a weathervane
he plodded through the air that touched the fishful water.
I followed him silently giving no quarter
all that afternoon. He never flew far from me
we kept meeting past each cape and estuary
but he always heaved doggedly out of touch. I
only wanted to stare myself into him to try
and thou him till we recognized and became each
other. We were both fishing. But I could not reach
his eye. He fled in puzzled ponderous pain
and I last rode home, conspicuous as Cain,
yet ashamed of a resigned demeaning pity

that denied us both. I returned to the city
and visited the zoo, fished on a concrete shore,
took children to aquariums, and rode no more.
I found that the encyclopedia says "A
gregarious bird. . ." No one spoke that desert day,
not one word. That fisher who heaved to dodge my eye
has damned himself an It and I shall never fly.

I

TO THOREAU ON REREADING WALDEN

> *I long ago lost a hound, a bay horse, and a
> turtle-dove.
> There too, as everywhere, I sometimes
> expected the visitor who never comes.*
> —Henry Thoreau

Your passion was ever plural, apart
from that one twig ("the twig") you never found.
Herds of birds and fishes, stars in droves
received your taut and tender gaze
but gills beaks planets can't reciprocate
and gratefully you prayed their praise.
You loved the faces in the fire, Thoreau,
the goldgreen pickerel, the huddling snow.
I too love these, and O love you, fierceheart,
and yet were you, like Lazarus, to rise,
you would look everywhere but in my eyes.
You'd hear the loud spring ice the greening ground,
but not the caller knocking at your gate
nor the nickering in your maple groves
nor the howling for home of the hound.
You did not listen to the turtle-dove
(singular bird) sing on your lintel: LOVE.
And now no visitor will come to crowd
Your peace. You have dried safely in your shroud.

AT THE ZOO

O the phoenix is gone and the unicorn
and the Chinese Nightingale.
No white whale blows
nor Persian rose,
the buffalo is robe and dust.

I have a headlong leaping lust
for zig and zag and hues and cries,
for the paradox of the musky ox
and the mute giraffe's embarrassed eyes.

One should not (in this zoo) throw down a glove.
It is the bars that shame a zebra out of love
and flinch the tender faces of giraffes
who stick their necks out and are good for laughs.
The beautiful the gentle the enraged
the strange the pitiful are shooed and caged
the preying cats and the shy kine who browse
on treetops. Peanuts are not thrown to cows.

If the buffalo quicken in his hide
and the phoenix rise and the virgin bride
lie with the unicorn
Roland's horn and Omar's rose and Moby Dick will blow
and every piper will be pied and cages will be never,
giraffes will wink and zebras prink and spring come on
        forever.

THE MASKED SHREW

> . . . *The Masked Shrew. . approximately one*
> *year of fastpaced gluttonous life.*
> — *Life Magazine*

A penny is heavier than the shrew,
dim-eyed and weaker than a worm
this smallest mammal, cannoned by a sudden noise,
lies down and dies.
No furnace gluttons fiercer than the shrew
devouring daily with relentless appetite
four times her inchling body's weight.
More extravagant than the hummingbird's the shrew's
hear beats per minute twice four hundred times.
If foodless for six hours she is dead.
The helpless, hungry, nervous shrew
lives for a year of hurly-burly
and dies intolerably early.

THE SLOTH

> *Body very hairy, tenacious of life.*
> —*Carl Linnaeus (1707-1778)*

Two centuries ago Linnaeus said "noise frightful, tears
    pitiful" of you,
bungled one. Arm over hairy arm you travel having no heels
to take to on your unsoled feet, no hole to hide in, and no
    way to fight.
Doomed to the trees, "good food for many," your one safety
    is in flight.

Today the scarce and lonely sloth, obedient prisoner in space,
astonished by perpetual pain looks askingly into my face
and hangs by legs and arms to life inexorably upside down
under branches in the zoo or in the subway under town.

THREE RINGS OR FIVE RINGS

Three rings or five rings no one would look for him in the
    main tent.
Where is the tendon and the soul to walk a rope
or even the tall cruelty to crack a whip
guts to heel-hang from a bar catch comrades from a dangled
    strand
brass to blare a horn, grace to crowd-wise tap music from the
    band?
He has not the muscled wit to juggle nor the accident
of beauty blood-rare and wild to prowl stage center in a cage.
Focused men who shove with pride sell cotton candy in the
    stands.
The calloused cautious roustabout takes pains with quick bare
    hands.
Punctual innocence sweeps the tanbark in between the acts
and humility leaps venerant to horses' schooled gay backs.

Clowns explode in pity and love (whimpers embarrass
    children into rage).
He is not caparisoned for the main tent. In the side-show
    mightily
he flirts adjusting his mock-mournful smile while cynically
    he poses there
cosily naked as though in his own parlor, a near herma-
    phrodite,
not a genuine freak but reason enough for our despair.

REVEILLE FOR A ROCKINGHORSE POET

Don't "trot trot to Bost-
on" child, gallop to Bordeaux.
Not every bell change has been rung
Nor every monster seen.
Hunt the Whale the Grail the Fleece
Kiss the cockatrice in Greece.

Don't "trot trot to market," child. Canter through Cockaigne.
Singlefoot to Samarkand and steeplechase in Spain
though far away translates to mean
(in the Zulu tongue)
"That place where someone cries out O
mother I am lost."

WHEN IN ROME . . .

It seemed a fine day for a canter.

The lady riding through the cattle corn
swung her right leg around the saddle horn
convinced the dun cow pony was a jennet
bell bridled flower wreathed and white as rennet.
The lady's breeches belled to a blue velvet habit featly
full; plumes brushed her cheek, her tasseled gloves moved neatly
through the ribboned reins. Dismounting by a willow tree
hung with mistletoe she sat upon the sandy sward,
gently expecting an encounter:
while around her the immodest birds exclaimed discordantly
reminding the still lady of her plight.

Alas too seasoned for the unicorn's bland appetite
the jeers of birds did disenchant her,
and straddling the bronco she loped home.

IN THE MUSEUM

Small and emptied woman you lie here a thousand years dead
your hands on your diminished loins flat in this final bed
teeth jutting from your unwound head your spiced bones
    black and dried,
who knew you and kissed you and kept you and wept when
    you died;
died you young had you grace? Risus sardonicus replied.
Then quick I seized my husband's hand while he stared at
    his bride.

ABRAHAM AND ISAAC

"Behold the fire and the wood but where is the lamb
for the burnt offering?" said little Isaac trembling.
"God will provide," said Abraham.

        Fathers of Isaacs cease dissembling.
        Will every thicket yield a ram?

COCK-A-HOOP

How struts my love my cavalier
How crows he like a chanticleer
How softly I am spurred my dear;
Our bed is feathered with desire
And this yard safe from fox and fire.
But spurless on the dunghill, dead,
The soldier's blood is rooster red,
His seed is spent and no hen fed,
Alas no chick of this sweet cock
Will speak for Christ at dawn o'clock.*

---

*When reprinted in *That Was Then: New and Selected Poems*, this poem was entitled "Cock-A-Doodle-Done."

II

IT RAINED LAST NIGHT

for John Logan

> *Nous n'irons plus aux bois,*
> *les lauriers sont coupés.*

Glass ponds astound the juicy grass, the air is wild
with the scents of thyme and fern and briny childhood
and the glistening birds call clearly in rinsed voices,
the sky is far and blue as a mariner's eye:
Listen, the greeness whistles . . .

O morning startling still and secret as a child,
a blue egg, as a moccasin in the wildwood —
O early day moving to afternoons of choices
I shall go once more to these woods until I die.
I know that the laurels grow.

20

WEST OF CHILDHOOD

for my brother, George Gardner

West of our childhood rote usurps the rites of spring, the
    wild sweet
season is an act of year. Uniformed robins hop and tweet
in chorus and culls from showgirls of seed catalogues doll up
    the view,
embellishing our Garden Homes, while Latin shrubs perform
    on cue.

    A child's fierce focused gaze can wholly enter
    and instantly become the bold gold center
    of a single crocus, a listening child is fused to the
        sole voice
    of that particular inimitable bird whose red choice
    breast is robiner than never, a child perceives
    the slow resolving of the one bud to the very leaf
        of leaves.

East of now and years from Illinois the shout of spring
    out-rang the dinner bell.
Brother do you remember the walled garden, our dallies
    in that ding dong dell
where my fistful of violets mazed the air we moved
    through and upon
and a swallow of brook skimmed your tabloid sloop to sea
    and gone?
North of tomorrow your daughter's daughter's ears will
    ding with spring, wild
violets will forest in her fist scenting towns of space; and
    my son's child

(weddings from this suburb) will, with crocus eyes, flower
    other Mays:
*That bud will leaf again, that choice bird sing, and paper
    boats sail down the robin days.*

FALL IN MASSACHUSETTS

I saw the tall bush burn.
(Nineteen times a gallows-tree . . .
The tongue of fire muted by our guilt. There cannot be
a voice for deaf New Englanders vowed never to be healed.)
I saw where a manna of flame had unfallowed the starving
    field.
           where a witch charred
           where her bones roared
where each of the good-wives took her choice of holiday or
    skewered house
and the mewing children barked another name
to their elders gathering apple-wood boughs
           and the sweet, the kindling fern:
           while cinders blew; and shame.

THE COMPLEAT ANGLERS

Wing fin and wrist bend wishfully
to cadences of summer noon
and courting lovers cast their bait
into the laden air of love.

The deft rod waits the still stream stirs
and mute gills tremble to the lure,
the lovers' taut hands listen to
soft nimble arias of love.

A ridden hawk screams like a cat
as hook is caught as mouth is reamed
as reeling lovers play their catch
through foaming areas of love.

CHILDREN ARE GAME

I have come often to this forest,
home to these never not green trees.
Now, in a grove of auburn bones
the spindling skeletons of summer flowers,
I hear the soft snow hiss through fir and spruce,
the shrill quick children skating on the pond
a safe and thousand miles from reef and shark.
What wings will whistle down this resined bark,
what monstrous blooming blast belief?
Children should not come to grief.
I swore that even crows could sing
I thawed my winters thinking spring
and now am always cold, with reason,
for bombs can blossom any season.
The pheasant's chicks scratch posted ground,
children are game the whole year round
skating the thin ice of the pond
gay and innocent and spruce:
while I in a grave of once-were flowers
and stiffer than their thready bones
forget these seen to be green trees
too mindful of the forest.

LINES TO A SEAGREEN LOVER

For Maurice English

My lover never danced with me
Not minuet nor sarabande
We walked (embracing) on the sand

My lover never swam with me
We waded to our ankle bones
And winced and shivered on the stones

My lover never flew with me
We stared at sea birds slicing space
And cried What freedom Look what grace

I wish my love had lain with me
Not on the sand beside the sea
But under my ailanthus tree

CADENZA

Conjure away the blue and the dim and the dark cloths
I am no longer in the night or in the half light
I want a shout of white an aria of fire
and a paean of green and a coral carillon
not Cinderella's slippers not the Emperor's new clothes
not the skull behind the flower but the bone that is the rose

GIMBOLING

Nimble as dolphins to
dive leap and gimble, sleek, supple
as ripples to slip round each other to
wander and fondle on under and into
the seeking and coupling and swarming of water
compliant as sea-plants to bend with the tide
unfolding and folding to frond and to flower
a winding and twining to melt and to merge
to rock upon billowing founder in surf
and a fathom's down drowning before the sweet waking
the floating ashore into sleep and to morning.

SUMMER EVENING

The salmon west leapt soft, spawned wild to sunset,
and the poaching lovers stood heron-still in the foam
of the orchard, baited to catch some sound of home,
while no dog barked and no door slammed and no child shouted.
But poplar leaves clashed like cymbals in the thin wind that blew
and at last the moon boomed out of the apple-tree and the two
lovers dove into the amorous dusk
and swam like swans through the clamorous air.

III

OF FLESH AND BONE

Child and girl each morning summer winter or dismay
my eyes saw waterfalls my ears heard madrigals I ta-
sted strawberries touched moss smelt hay and roses, and
    through the blue
the bright sky I with my first and once-love flew.
Willow-boned sun-marrowed and air-skinned,
sea-water in my veins, I drank wine and the southwest wind.
The noun death and the verb to die were exiled from my
vocabulary, and when the salty boys and sun-burned girls I
mooned with on the honeysuckled porch through locust-
loud and sigh-soft summer nights did speculate upon the
    disposition of my dust
I said to them I am a girl of flesh and bone, my shift's no
    shroud,
and d-e-a-t-h is the word I do not say out loud.
That is the word I said that I will not admit.
(I had read of a fatal Irish ghost name IT
who reeked corruption and whose gaze was potent as the
    basilisk,
and IT became my parlor slang for the noun I dared not
    risk)
The salty boys bugled desire to die at thirty-five
and the girls harped a lust to be buried, not old maimed
    and alive.
I vowed that eyeless earless loinless lonely,
I would refuse to die; that even if only
one sense was left me, touch or smell or taste,
I would choose to live; that in a sewer of waste
a thicket of pain a mountain of fear or the sea-
wrack of sorrow I would beg, steal, and betray to be.
Girl and child my nightmare was the ceasing,
not the attendant pinch and panic, but the releasing

of the I. Now that my blood's a sweeter blend,
now that my bones are bones and do not bend
now that my skin is dressed, what sucks my marrow
is not the final act of IT but the engagement some tomorrow.
The certainty, in spite of locking doors and looking in the
    closets, that *it* may wait
around That corner, under an unfamiliar bed, or through next
    summer's gate.
The meeting of ITS gaze in a sick second's shock of infinite
    danger
and then the slow or sudden but unrefusable embrace and the
    intolerable anger.
I am not faith-less but with those who see no future in
    eternity I do agree,
no paradise and no inferno will resolve the coming
    nothingness of me.
Mice and lions also die but God spared beasts our "knowing
    that we know"
today and yesterday, tomorrow, creeds and crimes ago.

Now mornings are still miracles and my dear now-love is
    my true
love and we fly we fly . . . O the sky was never once so
    bright and blue
and still I wish to live with living's theft-
ing and assault if even one sense will be left,
but to escape the meals and miles of waiting
I might elect the hour of my negating
and sleep peacefully to death some winter night,
cold finally to morning and to mourners and to fright.
Still, flesh and bone is wilful, and this knowledge is dead-
    certain and my horror,
that I shall not close my eyes when *its* eyes stare out of
    mine in every mirror.

HOMO GRATIA ARTIS

for Leighton Rollins

Ass-eared cross-gartered haloed crowned
Pearl-eyed and coral-boned and drowned
Victim-fathered son bride-mother
You are Abel and his brother
Eden Persepolis and Hell
Raskolnikoff and Philomel
The lamb the unicorn the goat
The burning shirt and Joseph's coat
The bleeding ear the bled-for nose
The apple mistletoe and rose
The pain the talon and the rock
You are the coffin and the cock.

THE LAST TRUMP

You suddenly squeak breathlessly like a squeezed rubber toy
you scream and scrabble in my kitchen, I am paralyzed.
You doomed freak of black and white you with your
    cockaded soul
self-freed self-housed and now self-trapped behind the
    hunching white
appliances that loom and glitter on the lunch-stained wall.
The reasoned breach between these units will not admit the
    most starved arm
or straining finger, no broom nor torch can bruise or burn or
    succor you
charity's green cheese is scattered on the waxed inlaid
    linoleum
(in death you smell the vinegared sponge) pragmatic mouse
    afraid to wait
for loaves and fishes, frightened to inch within a mouse-
    length of the bait
afraid to sleep inside the box contrived for you a grocer's
    carton
rag-padded, screened, stocked with a doll's dish of water and
    the choicest crumbs
to nourish you. Did you find freedom behind the stove
    icebox and sink?
Untemptable mouse, soon dead, and no one nothing can
    remove your stink
no light invade your coffin to focus on your rank ironic corpse
no dialectic can deny you. Your turd your bones your
    crucial shriek
will curd the lion's hollandaise, will thicken and goose the
    children's milk.

THE PANIC VINE

The panic vine quickens on the spine with the rise
and fall of every breath; and blooms inside the eyes.
A cold fruit bulges from the veins of wrists and arms
to bleed a virus juice into our sueded palms.
We spread disease when our gloved infrequent rites
of greeting are performed. If we exhume the roots
that lie in nightsoil bedded with the lungs of crows
roots watered by the coiled insistent garden hose
cold-framed against the thorn the analytic wind
the dazzling showers of the thundering sun bird blood
the grey goose feather and the white mare-mother's cud
if we expose these roots to weather and to wound
they would survive and we could bear the scattered rose
the spattered foal the honking flight and the sun's alms.

36

COWARDICE

The amputated human hearts pulse in the great glass jars,
As moist and wincing red as pigeon feet.

The jars will never be unsealed, nor can the heart be joined,
healed, to the breast. For in that vacuum, the fatal void
between the unreal and the real, between the brine and breast
the heart will burst. And we, compassionate, cannot redeem
the prisoned hearts, nor save the crippled men, the fear-
      oppressed,
who only suffer love within the prism of a dream.

THE MILKMAN

The door was bolted and the windows of my porch
were screened to keep invaders out, the mesh of rust-
proof wire sieved the elements. Did my throat parch
then sat I at my table there and ate with lust
most chaste, the raw red apples; juice, flesh, rind and core.

One still and summer noon while dining in the sun
I was poulticing my thirst with apples, slaking care,
when suddenly I felt a whir of dread. Soon, soon,
stiff as bone, I listened for the Milkman's tread.
I heard him softly bang the door of the huge truck
and then his boots besieged my private yard. I tried
to keep my eyes speared to the table, but the suck
of apprehension milked my force. At last he mounted
my backstairs, climbed to the top, and there he stood still
outside the bolted door. The sun's color fainted.
I felt the horror of his quiet melt me, steal
into my sockets, and seduce me to him from
my dinner. His hand clung round the latch like rubber.
I felt him ooze against the screen and shake the frame.
I had to slide the bolt; and thus I was the robber
of my porch. Breathing smiling shape of fright,
the Milkman made his entrance, insistent donor,
he held in soft bleached hands the bottled sterile fruit,
and gave me this fatal, this apostate dinner.
Now in winter I have retreated from the porch
into the house and once red apples rot where
I left them on the table. Now if my throat parch
for fruit the Milkman brings a quart for my despair.

TIMEO

Dear God (safe ambiguity)
If I address you faithlessly
the fear of heaven devils me.
Could I be sure of purgatory
Sure I could praise and not adore thee
I might a tepid faith embrace.
But I am terrified of grace.
Gethsemane is any place.

THE MINOTAUR

The labyrinthine forest's spoor
lead to the patient Minotaur
Deep in the dark and structured core
the bull-man waits inside the maze
and he who dares explore will raze
the beast of fear behind the door.

No Ariadne and no crone
will point the way. Each man alone
must thread his path, unreel his own
life spool and fumble to the lair.
Each man must journey naked there
nor arm himself with wing nor stone.

For he who goes his armor shed
and walks with all that once he fled
that man will face the horned head
the unimaginable eyes
and find there where the monster dies
the ichor that the terror bled.

THE ONLY RELIC

Hunting for coppers of Alaskan braves
in a forest of totem poles and graves
I found a skull no bigger than my eye,
greenish white, light as breath, and the only
relic there. I wondered who had to die
leaving just a bony scream and lonely
holes where eyelids blinked and no arms no loins.

Back home (with no beads no feathers no coins)
I hid the skull in a blue box with rings
I never wear these days and jagged things
crystal and turquoise I shall never mend
and moonstone cuff-links that I mean to send
back. The delicate anguished rigid shout
is still intact. But I shall take it out
now, place it on the mantelpiece, and wait
till children hide the fragments in the grate.

SOUTHWEST OF TRUE NORTH

Displaced by sandy distances
from tide and time and season,
detached from cadenced air and ballad
wind, from root and rime and reason;
shored where scarce water is voiceless
and ceaseless birds sing brashly out
of tune, beached in an alien landscape
a huge montage of drought
an impersonal district devoid of felicity
where neither the consonance of harmony
nor the complicity
of dissonance exists I loom and blunder
in a blast-bright land not by the grace
of God and suns evolved but conjured into ominous being.
In this assembled place
where matter hums with coiled intent
autonomous vitality
and no mineral vegetable animal or element
pertains to another; where no thing ripens or
decays, where life is reduced to existence
and existence to decor,
I find the birds especially intolerable.

These insolent incessant birds
loud bland indifferent feathered herds
as unrelated to this desert as the rocks and sand
as the cactus, creeks, creatures, weather, wind, and
I, yet breeding being dying in these regions
that I visit with a reaching eye; these gaudy legions
bold and practical as tourists,
flaunting detachment, wagging their
barnyard tails at my shocked seeking stare

twanging and harping as though I were not here
(as if to say
Don't bother with the salt tweak our tailfeathers any day . . .)
cocking a vulgar beak at me and my devotions
my barefoot Audubon-Saint Francis notions.

I cannot seduce these birds with love and a bread crumb,
nor startle them,
nor silently and undiscovered come
upon a thicket-full
to listen, concealed by my own care
and skill and will while they are singing
and unaware.
Never never can I approach them found
and finding to hear full frolic voices mute
to not a decibel of sound
till the perilous pause dissolving
resolves to a decimal dazzle of scale
a sheer precarious fluting of greeting
a flickering miracled carol of Hail.
North of this neighborhood I have been quickened by such
        canticles.
I am no guest
of these unbirdly birds. They are not disposed to manifest
concern with my immediacy. There is no benison or ban
from them to me. As though invisible I am not even an
intruder, am neither enemy nor friend,
have no identity.
Aroint thee birds
though hexed I am not your familiar. Nonentity,
I need a fang, a tusk, a talon, a bellow, a hiss, a roar
to un-bewitch me, one methodical
rattlesnake, an eager dinosaur,
an uncorrupted scorpion, a dedicated flea,
some single indigenous monster apt to acknowledge me.
Unlikely fantasy.

Not even the essence of evil is unalloyed
in this indecent territory,
the temper of the wildest beast is cloyed
to brisk neutrality.
No mythic wings whir down this shallow sky
to conquer these chimeric ciphers that neither listen nor reply.
I had expected residual souls in the local birds even at this
compass point. But environment is a factor difficult to alter
or dismiss.

> Birds in a vulnerable land
> where there is sea to salt the sand
> I rut, and roost, and rot, and sing,
> occasionally on the wing.

WHEN A WARLOCK DIES

for Dylan Thomas

When a warlock dies his rout of lemans, demons, fallen angels
and Familiars bend to the brewing of elegiac potions, fruity
    runes
plummed with their dead's distinctive spells,
mournful marketable meads composted of his rich remains.

As an apprentice witch, a mere familiar of Familiars, my
sunday-go-to-funeral broomstick (wreathed with mistletoe)
is handy to bestride in a cortege, to stir the baked meats, or to
    fly
a'wake-ing. Surely this deft-dirged, over-o-
ded, buzzard-hungry, heron-lonely, phoenix-hearted,
    gull-lunged
hummingbird-pulsed, falcon-winged and lark-tongued
Chanticleer has crowed his own Farewells and Hails.
And not all the ink and drink and spunk from Wichita to
    Wales
will wake this cock. The homage of our elegies whistles
    against the night
that looms too close for comfort since his death and our
    uncomfortable respite.

The roaring riming of this most mourned Merlin canticles his
    praise and His, and ours,
and Jerichos the walls of heaven with a surfing shout of love,
    and blasts of flowers.

THE LOOKING GLASS
(1961)

NIGHTMARE

A sleeping woman dreams she wakes
into a surging room of shrieks
and shapes. In the frantic room a red
haired woman looms . . . on her bent arm
there sleeps a girl's carved wooden head
A doll-sized nursing bottle nipples her huge palm
Both head and bottle drop and leeringly she
beckons. The dreamer screams her hatred
of the leering shape. Scrabbling for safety
the dreamer flounders on the floor.
The leerer pounces from behind the door.
The struggling dreamer stands
The dreamer lifts and clenches both her hands
The dreamer rips the red curls
in handfuls from that hateful head and hurls
the hairy gobbets at those manic eyes
The leerer dreadfully diminishes in size
She shrinks and shrinks into a little child.
The screaming dreamer beats the dwindling child.
The dreamer lifts a chair to smash that leering child.
Nothing at all remains. Not hag nor child.
No traces and no tokens.
The red-haired dreamer wakens.

48

THE WIDOW'S YARD

For Myra

"Snails lead slow idyllic lives . . ."
The rose and the laurel leaves
in the raw young widow's yard
were littered with silver. Hard-
ly a leaf lacked the decimal scale
of the self of a snail. Frail
in friendship I observed with care
these creatures (meaning to spare
the widow's vulnerable eyes
the hurting pity in my gaze).

Snails, I said, are tender skinned.
Excess in nature . . . sun rain wind
are killers. To save themselves
snails shrink to shelter in their shells
where they wait safe and patient
until the elements are gent-
ler. And do they not have other foes?
the widow asked. Turtles crows
foxes rats, I replied, and canned
heat that picnickers aband-
on. Also parasites invade
their flesh and alien eggs are laid
inside their skins. Their mating
too is perilous. The meeting
turns their faces blue with bliss
and consummation of this
absolute embrace is so
extravagantly slow
in coming that love begun
at dawn may end in fatal sun.

The widow told me that her
husband knew snails' ways and his gar-
den had been Eden for them. He
said the timid snail could lift three
times his weight straight up and haul
a wagon toy loaded with a whole
two hundred times his body's burden.
Then as we left the garden
she said that at the first faint chill
the first premonition of fall
the snails go straight to earth . . . excrete
the lime with which they then secrete
the opening in their shells . . . and wait for spring.
It is those little doors which sing,
she said, when they are boiled.
She smiled at me when I recoiled.

ZEI GESUND*

for Dr. Louis Cholden 1918-1956

In the preposterous sunlight
we watched them wincingly lower you
into your formal April grave.
In strict tears they tolled the Hebrew
litanies which (though you were not pious)
had wailed in the ark of your ear
and blown in the shule of your heart
as remindingly as Shofar.
You lived your life and died your death by
love, and if on that spring day you could
have spoken from the upholstered
isolation of your coffin, you would
have taken to yourself the sorrow
of your uncountable bereaved,
as you did always, possibly saying "that
I am the reason you are grieved
and that I cannot rouse to laugh you out
of tears distresses me as dying
can no longer." Louis, it is true
that when those loved do die our crying
is made most difficult to suffer
by the unstoppable sharing
of what we imagine to have been
the die-er's panic and despairing
in this ultimate encounter.
You spared us that pain, for knowing
your life-spirit robust past compare
we knew that you had braved your going
with your accustomed curiosity
and calm and courage. Every tear
is for ourselves, for our own loss,

the forever absence of you. Were
Death a hag (like those dishevelled
ladies in asylums whom you re-
deemed to dignity through your
accepting word and touch) I do be-
lieve you would have lent Ma Death a
comb for her lank locks and would fear-
lessly have stroked her fleshless shoulder
saying gently "Why Mrs. Bones, my dear,
haven't you come a little early?"
I think you would not have withheld
even from Death's self your thou-ing
greeting once you beheld
that incurable at your elbow.
You fought to keep her waiting for
you in the hallway while she
scratched and finally pounded on your door
but once she entered and that door closed
behind her you recognized the fact
of her outrageous presence and the
courtesy and courage of your heart listened intact
to her untimely undeniable demand.

It is not easy to remember that you died.
Neither your funeral nor our tears persuade
us, yet, that you have died. We shall confide
to you in phantasy through years of need
the flabby failure, shabby sin, and pride-
fully, the high Hungarian deed.
Our spirits shall by your quick soul be fed
until our bodies, too, are dead.

*Zei Gesund is a Yiddish phrase meaning literally "Be well"; it is used in
leave-taking; therefore: "Farewell." Shule is the Jewish word for temple; shofar,
for the ram's horn blown on the Day of Judgment.

IN MEMORY OF LEMUEL AYERS,
SCENE DESIGNER,
Dead of Cancer in His Fortieth Year

> *It is generall*
> *to be mortall*
> *I have well espied*
> *No man may him hide*
> *From death hollow-eyed.*
> —*John Skelton*

I that indulgently
am still allowed to be
address these lines to the
"Late Lemuel Ayers" who
did not elect to do
his dying young

Lem you are early late
Your life and death complete,
somewhere our dyings wait.
Finished with and by pain
you will not feel again
forgive us grief

Magical from the start
your strict and dazzling art
pure as your eye's taut heart
delicate bold and rare
castled the empty air
splendoring space

Truth-vizored knight of risk
vulnerable in your casque
magician of the masque

sword-wand in hand you strove
to conquer goat-foot's grove,
laurel your crown

Raped of felicity
ambushed unknowingly
by your bones' treachery
outraged by cone and knife
you labored for your life,
Myrtle, your wreath

Now you indulgently
observe our boon to be
alive and grieved, but the
shame is you've few friends who
dare to expect to do
their dying old.

ON LOOKING IN THE LOOKING GLASS

Your small embattled eyes dispute a face
that middle-aging sags and creases.
Besieged, your eyes protest and plead,
your wild little eyes are bright, and bleed.

And now in an instant's blink my stare
seizes in your beleaguered glare
the pristine gaze the blown-glass stance
of your once
total innocence.
I see and dare the child you were.

And for a wink's lasting, There
Now in your blistered eyes dazzles the flare
of Youth with years and love to swear
the kindling enkindled fire
heedless and sheer . . .
I see and fear the girl you were.

And now for a tic's lending, Now for the stint
of a second's fission I light to the glint
of your Daemon, that familiar whom you stint
so prodigally. Shunting, shan't-
ing, wincing fabricant
I see the maker that you want
and aren't.

And now just now I closed your eyes
your infant ancient naked eyes.
Gaze glare and flare and glint are buried by
my neutral eye-
lids. These island citadels are now surrendered
and with imagination's eye I see you dead.

56

"... AND THOU NO BREATH AT ALL?"

for Barbara Ransom Jopson, 1915-1957

Yours, Barbara, was a literal way of death.
You were defaulted by the failure of your breath.
To fox the taxing of your faltering breath
you schooled yourself for years to snare
a reasonable surety of air . . .
not surplus air to waltz or to embrace
just marginal sips to stay, with grace,
alight, and spark the hovering dark of death
with bright unwavering speech. You flogged your breath
down your dogged days and spent that wilting breath
in dialogues that burnished us with your
ungarnishable gold where we before
had counterfeited in our brass or gilt. Your art
was alchemy wrought by a sleight of heart.
That art will lend us gold beyond your death
and round the bend of our last breath
when we like you end, as we must, all out of breath.

SALOON SUITE

I. WALTZ FOR ACCORDION

The red balloon will collapse, my sweet
The snowman will melt in the sun
The daffodil dries on the hill
                              and
the kite blows away out of sight
But the hurdy the gurdy still giddies the street
                    and lilacs are BLOO-
                    MING in Kew
and the dancing the dancing
the rhyming romancing
will never no never be done.

II. JIG FOR HARMONICA

Murphy and company jig with Cohen
Shicker vie a Goy
Sing your slainthe landsmen
Lhude sing L'Chiam
Joy and joy and joy
and
Paesani   Please   It's time

III. TANGO FOR ZITHER

Loving you   Love   loving you
the least leaf
the least last lone-est leaf
redder is, red red   is redder
redder than   that maple grove
in fall   in fall in fall

58

                            and in
and in the spring   in the spring
the youngest and the littlest leaf
                   is green
a greener green a greenest green ah greener than
a willow tree
                   in May
in May in May
I love you, love you love   you far-
ther, than the farthest foam in
furthest most for ever wake of sea-
lost shallop
and more particularly Love,   than
the look! look looked-for shell than
the sought-found-shell than
the small and the whole shell's
sweet scallop.
Lost   love-lost   love-lost
I am lost Love I am lost love-lost
Love lost.
Sail me sail me home
Sail me sail me sail me home
My sailor   sail me sail me home
Reef me   steer me. Navigate me
home   home   home   home
home.

NOTE: This poem was written after hearing the "Third Man Theme," which should be kept in mind while reading Part II. "Shicker vie a Goy" is Yiddish for "drunk like a gentile," "Slainthe" is the Gaelic equivalent of "Here's to you," and "L'Chiam" is Yiddish for "slainthe." "Landsmen" is Yiddish for "fellow townsmen."

LITTLE ROCK ARKANSAS 1957

dedicated to the nine children

Clasping like bucklers to their bodies, books,
nine children move through blasts of killing looks.
Committed to this battle each child dares,
deliberately, the fusillades of jeers.
Their valor iron in their ironed clothes
they walk politely in their polished shoes
down ambushed halls to classrooms sown with mines
to learn their lesson. Obviously nine's
a carefully calculated number, odd
not even, a suave size that can be add-
ed to, discreetly, later, or culled now
should one child break not bend; or fail to bow
sufficiently his bloody head . . . a rule
to heed, child, be you black and going to school.

LETTER FROM SLOUGH POND

Here where you left me alone
the soft wind sighs through my wishbone
the sun is lapping at my flesh
I couple with the ripples of the fresh
pond water I am rolled by the roiling sea.
Love, in our wide bed, do you lie lonely?
the spoon of longing stirs my marrow
and I thank God this bed is narrow.

THE SEARCHLIGHT

From an anti-aircraft battery

In smug delight we swaggered through the park
and arrogant pressed arm and knee and thigh.
We could not see the others in the dark.
We stopped and peered up at the moonless sky
and at grey bushes and the bristling grass
You in your Sunday suit, I in my pleated gown,
deliberately we stooped (brim-full of grace,
each brandied each rare-steaked) and laid us down.

We lay together in that urban grove
an ocean from the men engaged to die.
As we embraced a distant armoured eye
aroused our dusk with purposed light, a grave
rehearsal for another night. The field
bloomed lovers, dined and blind and target-heeled.

MATHEMATICS OF ENCOUNTER

Two never-ever-will-be lovers each
thatched in a thicket of one-
liness, huddled in only-hood,
reach eye to perilous eye and contract
in an absolute gaze, in a clasping
of I's, a wedding. In that (ah marginal)
marrying of marrows, flesh blooms and bells,
blood shimmers and arrows, bones melt
and meld, loins lock.
In that look's-lasting love is resolved
to one-plus-one, dissolved again to two, these two absolved,
and the equation solved.

MEA CULPA

I do not love thee, Doctor Fell
The reason why I cannot tell
But this one thing I know full well
I do not love thee, Dr. Fell.

The plane rose loudly and rammed west
while I, as usual afraid, rejoiced
that the stranger beside me hid
the window's terrible view of our toy
enormous tinkered wing tilting
and shuddering out there
in the middle of the air.

I looked at the man by my side
and saw one eye, cheek, ear, and hearing air.
His tears fell out the eye and down the cheek.
Turning his head he fused his spilling gaze
to mine and begging angrily he said
"I am a surgeon hired to patch
the almost dead alive
but Doctor Fell will not arrive.

He is expected; and further
he is expected by the families
of the dying, who pay his monstrous fee
and fare, to be God Almighty's cousin . . .
whereas, clearly, I am not even
on time, lady, not even perhaps in
time, because a flight was cancelled." Knowing
him deaf I loudly cried
him grace, yelling, "You tried . . .
and they will know that you tried."

He mentioned trains and that they run on time
and that perhaps the waiting dying man
had died. "Yes, I am a surgeon," he said
softly, "but I had rather peddle used
cars to buy my beer. I am tired I
am tired of this frightful trust when I
confront and cut a bleeding carcass."
Touching his hand I blared
that the very *fact* that he cared . . .

"Care, care," he said as tears still slid
from his eyes, "can't you see I am not there?"
Abruptly he pulled a silver pill-box
from his pocket, and showing me his hands
and how they shook, he said, "I take a pill
at intervals to make my hands belong
and if I time the taking perfectly
these hands behave; they are golden, lady,
not one qualm or quiver in these
fingers, in these wrists, this heart,
or any other part."

I thought but could not bellow, yes, you care,
but the choice was yours; you made it leniently.
Your tears and pills and knives, my glib compassion
and my cadenced cant, these bleeding hearts
that blossom on our sleeves will not enlarge the
spirit, Doctor, nor reduce the spleen. We
must commit the act of caring before
indulging in elegiac tears. Our bills and
visits must be paid, our letters written,
our departures and arrivals made on time.
Trusting your weather eye
you assumed that plane would fly.

"Please forgive me that I have no comfort
for you . . . " I spoke out loud, but, not, it seemed,
quite loud enough, for he paid no heed, and
kneading his hands, remained silent until
our plane landed. I wished then to will him
well, but under the circumstances,
a resonant Good Luck struck me as flippant,
and a shouted Good-bye redundant.

SUMMER REMEMBERED

Sounds sum and summon the remembering of summers.
The humming of the sun
The mumbling in the honey-suckle vine
The whirring in the clovered grass
The pizzicato plinkle of ice in an auburn
uncle's amber glass.
The whing of father's racquet and the whack
of brother's bat on cousin's ball
and calling voices call-
ing voices spilling voices . . .

The munching of saltwater at the splintered dock
The slap and slop of waves on little sloops
The quarreling of oarlocks hours across the bay
The canvas sails that bleat as they
are blown. The heaving buoy bell-
ing *here* I am
here you are *hear hear*

listen listen listen
The gramophone is wound
the music goes round and around
Bye Bye Blues Lindy's Coming
voices calling calling calling
"Children! Children! Time's Up
Time's Up"
Merrily sturdily wantonly the familial voices
cheerily chidingly call to the children *time's up*
and the mute children's unvoiced clamor sacks the summer air
crying Mother Mother are you there?

PART OF THE DARKNESS

I had thought of the bear in his lair as fiercely free, feasting
    on honey and wildwood fruits;

I had imagined a forest lunge, regretting the circus shuffle and
    the zoo's prescribed pursuits.

Last summer I took books and children to Wisconsin's Great
    North woods. We drove

one night through miles of pines and rainy darkness to a
    garbage grove

that burgeoned broken crates and bulging paper bags and
    emptied cans of beer,

to watch for native bears, who local guides had told us,
    scavenged there.

After parking behind three other cars (leaving our headlights
    on but dim)

we stumbled over soggy moss to join the families blinking on
    the rim

of mounded refuse bounded east north and west by the
    forest.

The parents hushed and warned their pushing children each
    of whom struggled to stand nearest

the arena, and presently part of the darkness humped away
    from the foliage and lumbered bear-shaped

toward the heaping spoilage. It trundled into the litter while
　　we gaped,

and for an instant it gaped too, bear-faced, but not a tooth was
　　bared. It grovelled

carefully while tin cans clattered and tense tourists tittered.
　　Pains-takingly it nosed and ravelled

rinds and husks and parings, the used and the refused;
　　bear-skinned and doggedly explored

the second-hand remains while headlights glared and flash-
　　lights stared and shamed bored

children booed, wishing aloud that it would trudge away so
　　they might read its tracks.

They hoped to find an as yet unclassified spoor, certain that
　　no authentic bear would turn his back

upon the delicacies of his own domain to flounder where
　　mere housewives' leavings rot.

I also was reluctant to concede that there is no wild honey in
　　the forest and no forest in the bear.

Bereaved, we started home, leaving that animal there.

AT A SUMMER HOTEL

for my daughter Rose Van Kirk

I am here with my beautiful bountiful womanful child
to be soothed by the sea not roused by these roses roving wild.
My girl is gold in the sun and bold in the dazzling water,
she drowses on the blond sand and in the daisy fields my
    daughter
dreams. Uneasy in the drafty shade I rock on the veranda
reminded of Europa Persephone Miranda.

A LOUD SONG, MOTHER

for my son, Daniel Seymour

My son is five years old and tonight he sang this song to me.
He said, it's a loud song, Mother, block up your ears a little, he
said wait I must get my voice ready first. Then tunelessly
but with a bursting beat he chanted from his room enormously,
        strangers in my name
        strangers all around me
        strangers all over the world
        strangers running on stars
A deafening declaration this jubilant shout of grief
that trumpets final fellowship and flutes a whole belief.
Alone and in the dark he clears his throat to yawp his truth
that each living human creature's name is Ruth.
He sings a world of strangers running on the burning stars
a race on every-colored feet with freshly calloused scars.

Our stark still strangers waited back of doors and under beds
their socket eyes stared at us out of closets; in our heads.
We crawled on hob-nailed knees across our wasted starless land
each smugly thinking his the only face that wore a brand.
Sons, may you starve the maggot fears that ate our spirit's meat
and stride with brother strangers in your seven-league bare feet.

THAT PRINCELING

> *"Here is a candle to light you to bed*
> *here comes the chopper to chop off your head"*

That princeling bland with dapper smiles for daylit danger,
that dauphin gay as a dolphin at high noon,
in the purring night, pawed by the furry darkness,
howls mutely at the looming loneliness.

In his cold comfortable cage (unguarded)
bulging with beasts, pulsing with strangers,
in a ferocity of silence, it is his own
soft breath that pads and pants and pauses.

Bereaved and unbelieved, beset, be-nighted,
wincing from the awaited and insupportable pounce,
his little tender burrowing bones
bury him to bed.
    No lance no bow of burning gold
    No ewe no shepherd and no fold
    No jerkin of green nor coat of mail, no grace nor grail
    Can celebrate or succour him. Fearful and frail
that trembling desolate and dear prince cringes on his cot
while down unending corridors behind an arras (innocent and
    not
unarrogant with unicorns) the dauntless King and Queen
waltz sumptuously to sleep.*

*When reprinted in *That Was Then: New and Selected Poems*, this poem was
entitled "Bedtime Story."

CANZONETTA

for a god-son aged five

Swim little king-fish Leap small salmon
Sally from the sea and up the stream Fling
Game as Isaac and gold as Mammon
Plunge April fishlet Sprintheart dash
Drought's the drowning though love is rash
And anglers bait to poach your dreaming
  Cheat that larder, Beat that Chowder, Splash!

Gambol Gamble Easter lambling
Adam as Ram and mortal as Mother
Baa your benison Ding your damning
Bruise and blessing bell your bleating
Carillon lambkin rousing routing no retreating
Hurtle into wolf and spring's bell-wether
  Spiel your glock and, spell your flock, and Ring!

Gallivant giddyap bantam Will-joy
Bold as bugle and brave as bunting
Trumpet! Furl out! Bannering boy
Gallop to the hill-top. Strut your stride
Raising praising choosing losing never hide-
ing, heeled by the hope that hounds your hunting
  Sound your horn Astound your dawn and Ride

NOT AT ALL WHAT ONE IS USED TO . . .

for Frances Pole

There was never any worry about bread or even butter
although that worried me almost as much as my stutter.
I drank coffee with the others in drugstores and then went
back to my room for which I paid a lower rent
than I could afford and where I was proud
of the bedbugs, and where I often allowed
myself an inadequate little Rhine wine. Two
or three times a week after seeing the producers who
were said to be looking for comedy types I wandered
off to the movies alone and always wondered
if anyone in the mezzanine knew me by sight, or might
know me by name or have kissed me and I felt an itch
to stand right up and ask, like swearing out loud in church.
Only one agent agreed to be rude to me every day, a
cross cockeyed woman who had acted in her youth.
I was not union because I had never been paid and the truth
is no other agent would speak to me or even see me until I
     was Equity . . .
a vicious circle but not unpleasing to me.
I smoked for hours in producers' anterooms where
I prayed that interviews I had come there
to beseech would be denied.
Usually my prayers were granted and I stayed outside.
I was a tense imposter, a deliberate dunce,
in a lobby of honest earnest seekers. Once
or twice thanks to a letter of introduction I
got to see the man, but instead of "chin up" and "do or die"
I effectively slouched and stammered in disorder in order
to thus escape the chance to read I might be
offered. An English director once said I was the
"perfect adorable silly ass," due in part to a part

he saw me do in which I had to lisp and giggle.
But that of course was in another country. I did not boggle
at summer stock, and somewhere north of Boston I had
at last become a paid member of a company where sad
to relate I was successfully grotesque in numerous unglamourous
bit parts (usually dialect for I did not stutter
in dialect) and I was always differently grotesque, utter-
ly; but people laughed and/or cried, always saying I was play-
ing myself, that I was a 'natural'. Through the good offices of a
well-connected friend I at last read for a producer who was
        Broadway
and was given the part of a Cockney maid, afraid
and eager, who moved and talked in double-time.
But I was fired. The stars complained for no rime
or reason that they became confused when I was 'on' (there
        was no basis
for their saying that the audience laughed too much and in the
        wrong places)
although it is possible that I just did everything faster and
        faster.
I had come to depend on the laughs and dismissal was a
        disaster.
My next job was a haughty lady's maid with a faint brogue
and a strip-tease walk. One night (in Hartford) I was more
        rogue-
ish than usual and the college boys broke up the show
banging their feet on the floor and whistling. Not long ago
I portrayed a madwoman (but gentle and sentimental)
I curtseyed, sang a short song as I did not
stammer when I sang, and fondled a telescope that
had belonged to a sea-going ancestor. It was agreed
that at last, despite previous successes, I had indeed
and finally found my niche. It was declared
that I could go on and on doing that kind of thing, but I dared

myself to attempt only straight parts although it is hard
    (playing with fire)
for a character actress to play herself and only too true
that the audience response is not at all what one is used to.
Nevertheless it is a challenge and no reason to retire.

SUMMERS AGO

for Edith Sitwell

> *The Ferryman fairied us out to sea*
> *Gold gold gold sang the apple tree*

Children I told you I tell you our sun was a hail of gold!
I say that sun stoned, that sun stormed our tranquil, our
    blue bay
bellsweet saltfresh water (bluer than tongue-can-tell,
    daughter)
and dazed us, darlings, and dazzled us, I say that sun
    crazed
(that sun clove) our serene as ceramic selves and our noon
    glazed cove,
and children all that grew wild by the wonderful water shot
    tall
as tomorrow, reeds suddenly shockingly green had sprouted
    like sorrow
and crimson explosions of roses arose in that flurry of
    Danaean glory
while at night we did swoon ah we swanned to a silverer
    moonlight than listen or lute,
we trysted in gondolas blown from glass and kissed in fluted
    Venetian bliss.

> Sister and brother I your mother
> Once was a girl in skirling weather
> Though summer and swan must alter, falter,
> I waltzed on the water once, son and daughter.

WRITING POETRY

for James Wright

is one game that no-one quits while he or she's ahead. The
stakes are steep. Among the chips are love fame life and
    sanity.
The game's risk is that winning one chip often means the
    forfeit
of another but despite the penalties there is a surfeit
of players. Some are only kibbitzers, others play it safe
(their chips are counterfeit) cheating, they may not come
    to grief,
or so they hope, and hoping keep their places near the pot.
There are other gambits deployed to trick the croupier's hot
eye and hand. For some in terror for their reason and their
    rhyme
There's a disguise in style to rent or borrow or assume:
hair-shirts, brocaded waistcoats (the gilt is slightly tarnished)
sackcloth interlined, embroidered chasubles refurbished,
helmets turbans caps (with bells) wreaths high silk hats
    cockades . . .
and for women Quaker bonnets wimples coifs and sunshades,
long blue stockings hawking gloves a fan a hobnailed boot.
But it's the gamblers wearing their own hides who shoot
the moon rocketing on unprotected feet to outer space
where (out of pocket, having no sleeves up which to hide
    an ace)
they fall bankrupt or being down to their last chip are stran-
ded. No-one has pocketed the moon since the game began . . .
or . . . sooner than they did
they died.

JEAN SANS TERRE
WRAPS HIMSELF IN A RED COAT

Coming toward you in my red coat
Do not ask me if I wear the mantle of the king of Tyre
Or the cloak of the beggar of Benares
My coat is lined with love

The song of love goes before me as crimson dust
Preceded the sirocco which trails the sulphurous storm
It breathes above the seven couching hills
Before astounding the valleys of thirst dried up by Satan

For it is a wind of anger that swells my bloody coat
And flares my pine torch from the forest's depths
I carry vengeance to the people who still dream
In the strangled slums, in the hangars of nightmare

In the flophouses of the Beggar's Court
In the bazaars where hang the carpets blood-stained
By the thousand-year-old hand of slaves
In the prisons cemented by tears and petrified skulls

I light I light with my dancing torch
The tarnished skies of the cities
For the poor who exist on the thirst of others
And have not the right to be thirsty

Those who peddle the song of apples
Of milk of rain of air and the coca of the Trusts
Those who sell exactly enough to die
To dress the abscessed wounds of their children

I come I come on my red horse
Whose wings are put together with flaps
Torn in strips from my heart, from my vagabond's coat . . .
His hooves flower the rock to a rosebush of love

His nostrils breathe fire from the stars to you
I come from the depths of the forever virgin forest
And I kindle for you all the birds of my crown
The fire of the lyre-bird and the golden fire of the phoenix

A universal Saint Elmo's fire
To spark men's dust
To portion joy to all the corners of the world
To wrap you, my brothers, in a crimson coat

— *Yvan Goll*

JEAN SANS TERRE
THE CHEST OF DRAWERS

I am a chest of drawers
Open to the passerby
Containing enough to eat and drink
And above all to die

Here is the bunch of mouldering keys
The bouquet of keys to fields and dreams
Here is the key which locks the door of grace
And the one which will open my tomb again

In this drawer I have the essence of rain
And the spices of the earth
Pepper for killing memories
And shadow — dissolving salt.

In another a gold ancestral watch
The watch time cannot break
Anger Love Nothing stops it
No hammer shatters this dial

Here is the keen edge to sever trust
The wool for mending friendship
But alas I have dropped the stitch
Which could re-weave the wing of innocence

The pack of cards from which my wife emerged
The accountings which prolong the lunar year
And my will written in invisible ink
Will see the notaries of Tartar age.

This compass measures the angle of sincerity
And this bell pings for every lie
And here is a life-supply of nails
To crucify the guilty.

There I have the bleached heart of my mother
Who always knitted socks for the condemned
And I have the ivory hand of my love
Lost as she leaned to wave farewell

The seventh drawer contains the tools of prayer
The gimlet for the worm of temptation
The file against the growth of improvised thoughts
And the pliers to screw tight the piety of my hands

> I am a chest of drawers
> Locked from the passerby
> Containing enough to doubt and trust
> And above all to die.

— *Yvan Goll*

WEST OF CHILDHOOD
(1 9 6 5)

ROUNDELAY

A blood-red bird with one green eye
and one gilt wing is hanging high.
Slung by the neck on a Christmas tree
dangling there in the tinsel he
is not about to sing for me.

The tree it trembles, the glass gauds swing
like that bird with his one gilt wing
who bows his beak, whose one eye glows
as back and forth and round he goes
to grace notes and arpeggios.

THIS ROOM IS FULL OF CLOCKS

I am trying to write at a desk that is mine
these mornings thanks to the kindness of a stranger.
His room is full of clocks. All of them are ticking.
I fumble through a folder of abandoned poems
and of news stories I cut from papers I must
have conned some enterprising morning years ago.

Here is the account of a rare black swan that flew
from somewhere to Waukegan Harbor to a Greek
cafe where "it huddled at the door its feathers
drenched with oil." The swan was sad reports the paper,
        so Mathon
Kyritsis, restaurant keeper and fisherman,
consulted an ornithologist who said the
sorry bird was one of one hundred nineteen Black
Australian Swans that still survive and that the bird
could not live in captivity without its mate.
No doubt this Rare Swan died of fatigue let alone
bereavement even before I snipped the clippings.
Perhaps Mr. Kyritsis lives telling his tale . . .
The paper did not give the age of Mathon K.

Here's a clipping with the heading ANIMALS:
HOW OLD THEY GET. It is an accounting from the "the
reliable records of zoos, aquariums
and aviaries all over the world," offered
with comments by the Cook County Forest Preserve.
For instance it says here that "man is longer lived
than any other mammal," and sure enough the
record shows a pampered elephant only made
it to sixty-nine. It is different for some
of our poets. MacNeice and Roethke have died

at fifty-five just like the Giant Salamander
while an occasional catfish is alive at
sixty. I don't begrudge the turkey-buzzard his
one hundred and eighteen years, nor the swan who if
he has his mate can live to one hundred and two
(that rare Black Swan who flew to Waukegan did not)
but I mind reading that coddled alligators
(safe from such random killers as love or neglect)
are able to thrash and lash and grin at sixty-eight.
Even in these days not Thomas, Cummings, Roethke
or MacNeice have managed that. It is possible
that there should be a Forest Preserve for poets
each with his or her mate but I remind myself
that the poet is rumoured to be less constant
than the swan. No the bard must do his best with book
and bed and booze and blunders of the heart and
bearing witness burying friends banning bombs
and using onomatopeia with restraint.

A WORD FROM THE PIAZZA DEL LIMBO

for William Congdon

Infrequently but massively I hear
from one who until recently seemed crammed
with *caritas*. Now, since the saving of his
soul his letters speak only of himself and
of Him and of their correspondence.
Indeed he declines to address himself to my
distress. Although I have written him of
various despairs he does not even
upbraid me for Sloth, the sin with which
I wake and eat, that monkey on my back.
I realize that right this minute he may
be praying for me (though fretfully, the
way one writes a postponed letter, I MUST
pray for Belle today) because being yet
but a fresh-washed lamb he is bound to be
nervous about wasting God's time, and of
course his own which I can well understand.
I can also see that he has his own
chores if only, for Heaven's sake, keeping in
good with God, with whom he has a close but
complicated relationship, while I at present
lack even a genuflecting acquaintance.
Not God's fault God knows. I have avoided
Him since losing innocence. I do not
say evaded because though arrogant,
I cannot imagine that He has been
loping breathlessly after me all these
years hoping to heal me and herd me to
the fold. When I was a clear-eyed child,
reading about Artemis and Snow White,
I secretly got down on my knees when

the light clicked out and my brother and I
had said our I Lay Me's and been kissed.
We slept on a screened porch almost out of
doors. In winter the bare floor was arctic
and I made certain that my knees were bare.
Then (a confirmed believer in my own
omnipotence) I prayed and prayed
for the maimed the halt the blind the hungry,
for every category of misery
that I could, in innocence, imagine.
No syllable of my petition ever varied
lest that deflect my power to persuade.
Yes, I was magical then. I could fly.
When I climbed a tree I put my arms round
the trunk and my ear to the bark and heard,
faintly, the dryad speaking, and I had the evil eye;
and the Unicorn's head once lay in my lap, and bareback
I galloped Pegasus. I moved Mt. Monadnock.
I walked across blue Mt. Hope Bay. I believed.

I lived too long a time in innocence,
but not quite long enough to wholly make break or addle
me. A critic wrote "the pilgrim for whom no chapel
waits." But still I wear the scallop shell
and shall till I go down the well
                    Ding   Dong   Belle

THAT WAS THEN
(1980)

I
THE ACCOMPLICES

THE ACCOMPLICES

Must now accomplish the division of remains.
Assassins they will now be scrupulous
take pains to be exact in the division of each part
(Let not the question of the genitals impede
the disposition of their singular dead.)
Each must be left with half a
head and half a heart a hand
for him a hand for her a lung apiece
and an iambic foot for each and then surcease.
As to the disposal of the parts his portion
will rot in the attic carried there
and then forgot. His half the heart
plopped in an Etruscan jar they bought in Tuscany
the rest of his share he will lock in a trunk
her half a heart she will pound in a mortar
and eat. The rest of her share
will be burned until charred black.

WHO SPILLED THE SALT?

They both spilled the salt. No doubt about that.
No accident . . . it was collusion.
It looked crystal clear from where I sat.

Though I couldn't *quite* see around Sister Anne's hat
and there might have been some collision.
They both spilled the salt. No doubt about that.

They did it together, tit for tat
though it might have been an illusion
it looked crystal clear from where I sat

and nobody seemed to smell a rat
so it surely was not a delusion?
They both spilled the salt? No doubt about that

as nobody thought to send for the cat.
Though there *might* have been some occlusion
it looked crystal clear from where I sat.

And so though it sounds a little too pat
I shall have to repeat in conclusion . . .
It looked *crystal* clear from where I sat.
They both spilled the salt. No doubt about that?

SALT

If the salt hath lost its savour
wherewith shall it be salted?
—Matthew 5:13

The ocean is salt and the waters
of the womb. Sweat is salt and tears. Pure
salt was poured in sacrificial slaughters

by high priests of Israel. Salt was the cure
for and against corruption of spirit and flesh,
salt sprinkled at baptism and burial to make sure

that Satan would be reticent. Scots kept their mash
from the taint of witches by seasoning the malt.
In Athens, Attic salt gave sage discourse its dash.

My love: Ours was not "a covenant of salt,"
therefore I rub salt in our common wound
to scourge us for our kindred sins and kindred fault.
You rowed me up Salt River: but I'm on dry ground.

II
PART OF THE DARKNESS

COCKCHAFER:

. . . greyish-chestnut beetle flying with
loud whirring sound.
— Concise Oxford Dictionary

Desist Cockchafers: You Kamikaze Beetles of June.
What a chafing relentless cocky crowd of whirrers
you are! I massacre you one by one
and by the dozen but back you Whirr
and CRUNCH go your hard foolish
beetle-bodies as I take aim and flail
at your Whirrs with the flat of an aging shoe
Whack and you're dead. Crack, you too.
Smack as you hit the floor and Whirr
fly your cousins and your uncles and your aunts
zizzing straight at me, a myriad of Whirrs.
Stealthily I put on the light and wait, sitting
upon the sofa bed (humming my silent menacing hum) grasp-
ing my beetle-scarred shoe in my guerilla hand
        I have to ERASE you.
At the first attack-wave I'd employed a simple shout
Get OUT! AVANTI! RAUS! no use.
Ergo, combat to the death; all of you.
All through the night I am besieger and besieged.
        At last silence, and sleep.
I wake to 19$^1/_2$ corpses. Some squished flat. Those
still twitching mine the floor. I put on solid shoes
and stamp on you cocky twitchers CRUNCH
Crunch-crunch, and sweep you up,
and out. Alright you had the right, horrendous beetle-dom
to try and patch your wounded and pack up your dead
But I'll NOT have you whirring around & around
the air-port of my hair and crashing in my head.

THE MOTH HAPPENED

For Jay Bolotin

The moth happened, Jay.
I say it, she, he, *happened.*
I'd read your letter, was thinking of you
I was walking toward dinner and
thinking of you. I had a glass of wine
in one hand a straw satchel in
the other. Instead of looking up
at subtleties of mist and sunset
I kept my eyes where my feet
placed themselves. I looked for mica
for a flat sliver of mica I could mail you,
and I saw a palpable moth quivering on the path.
I gently dropped my glass of wine. I stooped
to you Moth. I held out my hand
held a hand gingerly tenderly under you.
I stood up. There you were on
the back of my hand. I breathed to you
stay there, hold still dear moth
dear moth I love you love you
you were velvety deep deep black,
your wings bright white, so *white* . . .
and edged with a laciness of white.
When the sounds and lights of dinner
were upon us you began to fan your wings and
then to beat your bright white wings, until you,
lighter than a thistle's down, had flown a flight
into the hawthorns and away from noise and light.

III
HOMO GRATIA ARTIS

YOUR FEARFUL SYMMETRIES

for Alice Neel

> *The hidden internal structure of the tiger*
> *may be unknown to us, but it is the essence*
> *of the tiger.*
> — *Noam Chomsky on Saul Kripke*

The anger of loving
the ferocity of survival
those vulnerable cocks
    which you expose
the mothers whose faces
are frightened by their love
of the naked faces of their
trusting children who expect.

Whether you, Alice Neel, assess
define or collect souls

it is the internal structure
    that matters.
I saw a portrait I saw a
man's brain bulge through his eyeballs
I saw nerve ends supplanting
bones in his prehensile hands
the upper face a scholar-priest
a jovial smile that bared the teeth:
    a rictus.

To be able to love
and to be alive
witness is proof
anger is necessary

    Tyger Tyger Burning Bright.

THE TELEPHONE

— The prefix tele means in Greek far away

The telephone rang
in my dream Long Distance from
my dead father

Impersonation?
Who and why? The voice was his
my dead father's voice

dead a month ago
I'd turned sixty-one Mother
I was bewildered

in my dream I asked
what think you brothers sisters?
I wondered and I woke.

THE MUSIC ROOM

You must never unlock the cedar closet,
Nor open the white doors to the music room
To be stared at by the french windows and drained
Flabby by the sucking mouths of pastel plants
Unseasonably bred, denatured, deformed.
There in the corner crouches the piano

That vibrates pianissimo piano
And crescendoes con amore in the closet
Of your mind, there by agons of time deformed
And dimmed, but resonating, leaving no room
For any theme but dread. Behind the white doors plants
Alone were smiled at, but with joyless pride that drained

Odor and pollen. It was indifference drained
The marrow from the bones of the piano,
Gutted the child, but watered the tuneless plants.
Only camphored clothing hangs in the closet
No souvenir, no clue to another room
Paper sealed the clothes are tidily deformed.

Go away, do you think you can be deformed
Only once in the same way, that once drained
You cannot be drier? Play the piano
Louder than the echoes of pain but the room
With the staring windows will again closet
You with the chords of terror and the deaf plants.

O multiply impotent is he who plants
His target heel on these thresholds so deformed
By strangled battles that the air is drained
Of sustenance as a sealed up closet,

As the tense unplucked strings of a piano.
Step back. There has been blood in the music room.

Totem's whistle skirled and dwindled in this room
Of slaughter. Rosily embalmed the corpse plants
Frill the bald windows behind the piano.
The keyboard grimaces at the most deformed
Of all, at him who snail-wise wears his closet
On his back; the leech by which his veins are drained.

Drained child, child still, you are buried in this room.
Embalmed like the plants, hanging in the closet.
Mute in hate as the piano, and deformed.

ARE POETS BALL PLAYERS?

Marianne Moore loved baseball
                    She was a winner
I loved Marianne but that's a nothing
answer to question marks in a title
                    No equations
                    Few convictions
                    Some con victims
                    Rarely ever opinions
                    Can our perverted
language yield possible idioms or
jargons of trade: baseball's trade for instance?
Baseball's language exists uncorrupted
                    As "Who's On First"
                    and not who is first.
                    Next question is Who
                    is the Catcher in
                    The Little Jacky Horner Pie?
Biggest question: who is playing Short Stop
Not the late Rabbit Maranville, not these
days, but Short Stop is the nitty gritty and
maybe the ploy's still around: that double
                    play "from Tinker to
                    Evers to Chance" in
real life you cannot count on tinkering
                    for evers or chance
                    That's risky and that's
                    stoopid, Lucy knows
                    Snoopy doesn't, he's
an anachronism, a risk taking loser
who *likes* himself. Some of us rabbits are chicken
"There's nobody here but us chickens and none of
us is Rabbit. We wait out in Left Field

Where is that Fly Ball
It's lonesome out here
Way out in Left Field
and if we come up to bat along with
Charlie Brown old Uncle Tom Cobbler and all
we don't know when to
bunt, but swing at each
pitch with might and main
and mighty sorry aim
aiming to swat the pitcher's incurve out
of sight. The Umpire like as not will strike
us out. The Umpire
never calls Foul Ball
The Umpire's not about to Walk us
There are no free Walks for Poets to first
base on balls. The Umpire counts and chooses
So we Warm the Bench, jounce back to Left Field
or, maybe, we touch all three bases and
slide in peril to Home Plate
That Home Run at last.

(Allee Allee in free?)

IV
THAT WAS THEN

CARD ISLAND OR COD ISLAND?

I did not know then and I do not know now.
The child I was went there nearly every night for a winter
or more, half a century ago. My younger brother George
slept in the same room. The muttering embers
in the grate spoke quivering pictures to the ceiling.
What a viewing! From these slipping shapes I construed
a hill-side coastal village and staring hard I was transported
to that primal coast I stood on the pier I climbed the steep
      street.
All the cobblestoned way up that hilly street every single
tiny house was full of light. The little houses all alight
by the light of whale oil lamps. All doors ajar. HERE you
All the people in their houses shouted here you ARE
Here's cookies, ginger people baked for you Here's a
      BOTTOMLESS
pitcher of milk for you. From each glowing little house
they beckoned me and they welcomed me and they hugged me.
I was theirs. They were mine. Such Love!
      Wolves bared their teeth at my little brother in his dark.
Only to my father each bedtime, and to our Irish laundress
those mornings she was there, did I recount the serial tales
of where I'd been and gone. George, two years littler than I
cried "Take ME Take ME why can't I
go too?" How could I answer him? The laundress, crisp
and tactful Celt, asked me "and who was it then that
you saw *last* night, dear?" I'd tell her. She would nod.
It was understood between us that she'd been there too and
      knew
the Island and each Islander. "Give my love to all,"
she'd bid me. If I missed a night of going there
she'd say "Well now dear I couldn't make it myself last night.

They'll know we both had other fish to fry."
Cod Halibut Haddock Scrod
In the afternoons my mother played Cards
Scrod Haddock Halibut Cod
At my bedtime my father played God
The King the Queen the Ace the Jack
I was the joker in the pack
Island Island Cod or Card
Once your coast was my backyard.

FEELING OF TIME

And when the light is exact
And only the shade of memory falls
Across the little peak that is no Alp,
In the distance bared by perspective I face the past,
My pulse as usual beats, in accord with heart's habit,
But now I listen to it,
And Time, I hurry you, harry you and would marry you,
Time, to our final embrace.

—Giuseppe Ungaretti

KNOWING

> *Mon moi, Ils m'arrachent mon moi*
> *— Michelet*

I will be lonely at half past dead
Weep none one or many beside my bed.
At the dead center of all alone
I must unwillingly work at dying
I will be crying crying crying
Not I not I this flesh these bones.

COLLAGE OF ECHOES

For Elliott Coleman

I have no promises to keep
Nor miles to go before I sleep.
For miles of years I have made promises
and (mostly) kept them.
                    It's time I slept.
Now I lay me down to sleep
With no promises to keep.
                    My sleeves are ravelled.
                    I have travelled.

PROSPERO'S ISLE

For Emil Hodge

They don't smoke pot
They booze a lot
They fight cocks
And with a big cupped hand
They check their crotch
But the sound of the sea was incessant
I just couldn't take it
They're every color of the rainbow
So they have no color problem
(I got sick there flat on my back
For a whole week)
I'm going to rest in Boston
And then
By God I'm going back
I'm going back
Come hell or high water
That damned place
I love it so

Grand Cas., St. Martin

BRONCHITIS AT THE CHELSEA
—OR SALUD RAUL

for Raul Caraballosa

My chest hurts every breath I draw
The Cuban snores upon the floor—
His beautiful blue and bloodshot eyes are closed
His colossal belly overflows.
He tends me tenderly, alert
to the hour of each prescribed pill's taking—
He poultices my chest with steaming towels
and he simmers honey and lemon juice to
anoint my vanquished voice.
Today at my beseech he came
with me to the airport. We ate and drank.
He waved goodbye.
Too far gone is he in booze to truly care
but he will miss me for a while.

Postscript

Raul I flew back
to California and I packed
up my life there. I flew back
to you. You had walked into a truck
while my plane flew. Your skull cracked
You died not knowing I flew back
not knowing the racking
sobbing of the man whose truck
your undirected body attacked.
At the funeral parlor your mother rocked
Aiee Aiee she cried but never cracked
Nor loosed the easier tear. Raul you can't come back.

THAT WAS THEN

for Riva Blevitsky

Union Pier Michigan. We called it Shapiro
Shangri La. People said I needed a passport.
I was the only Shicksa there Kolya Shura
Manya Tanya and Sonya, Sulya Myra and
Vera they were there. And Riva a young girl then.
Soda pop and ice cream parlors, no bars,
Delicatessens but no liquor stores.
They spoke fractured English fractured Yiddish
and fractured Russian when they did not want
their children to understand. Most husbands
drove down from Chicago fridays but mine
came to me thursdays bringing the squat green
bottles of Chilean white wine I drank
(he was angry if I forgot to buy
cucumbers) My daughter then five, now in
Bedlam, chased butterflies and thirty years
ago my infant son, now for some years
lost, was happy too. I washed his diapers
in a tub and hung them up in the sun.
Instead of a play-pen, my husband, Seymour,
called Simcha which means joy, made a paddock
for him. Dan did not like to be cooped up
(nor did Rose, my daughter Rosy; nor did she)
not then, not later, never. Dan was last
seen in Columbia, South America.
Simcha little Rosy littler Daniel
and the Shicksa we were all of us joy-
full then in Shapiro Shangri La when
we were young and laughing. On the lake beach
the women waded and gossiped. The men,
supine on the hot sand sucked in the sun

through every work and city tired pore
and on the blithe beach played chess needling each
other, "singing" they called it. The Shicksa
swam and her daughter, round pink Rosy made
castles out of sand and when the big rough
boys' unseeing feet crushed her battlements
she cried. (As she would later, as she did
later, as she does now and must again
in inexorable time.) Ah but then
it was different. The first summer at our
Michigan Shangri La we shared one half
a cottage with Seymour's sister Molly
Molly the matriarch and my mother
too Molly amply Yiddish mama
bountiful heart bountiful flesh married
to tender Ben Blevitsky book-binder
and Bolshevik, not Communist though he
thought he was and paid his Party dues.
He pressed on me, a bemused fellow traveller
The Daily Worker which I occasionally
scanned. Aside from Ben's misguided fealty
to a party that betrayed his each, his
every dream, he taught the Shicksa wisdom,
ancient Hebraic, of the heart and pulse.
This Shicksa loved him all his life. He died
attacking Zionists. In the debate
the heckling hit his heart and aged eighty-two
gentle Ben Blevitsky fell down and died.

That first summer the Shicksa shared the stove
with Molly who wouldn't let her cook
a meal but did teach her to cook kugel
and fix gefilte fish. (It was only
the Shicksa's second marriage and so she
had not yet lost her appetite for cooking,
that came after the fourth marriage when

she recklessly played house with a fifth man.)
Political not pious there was not
kept, a kosher kitchen. Molly and Ben
once took the bus to Chicago saying
they'd be back saturday night for supper
saying Be well Bellotchka but don't cook!
Later Molly cheeks streaming with laughter
crowed to cronies "The Shicksa cooked a haser
for the Shabbas!" Stuck with cloves it was,
the scored cuts thumbed full of dark brown sugar
hot powdered mustard and the fresh squeezed juice
of sweet oranges and the whole ham smeared
with that luscious mixture and therewith glazed
and all ate that haser with high delight
the Blevitskys, Molly, Ben, and their Bob and Riva
Rose, Simcha and his Bellotchka—the cook
ate and ate while the infant Daniel slept.

That was then. That was then.

UNCOLLECTED POEMS

BALDUR WAS BEAUTIFUL TOO

I love I love I love and oh
am loved by him whom I love so.
Love has no ease because I know
Love's seed, Love's blood dyes alien snow.
I dress in black, a tearless crow
and pin my heart with mistletoe.

SONNET FOR MY ACQUAINTANCES

I love not me but what you see and for
This pittance I have myself denied my
Self admittance. You thought my heart an open door
And you rushed in and never knocked and I
Did not seek why you never even tried
To look in windows or to ring the bell,
To wait, polite, till asked to come inside.
You called to all your friends when night fell
Then I called too and with more force than you.
Come in and eat and warm your hands I shouted.
You came and there was nothing I could do.
I did not know when I myself was routed.

Because I let the key-lost door stand wide
There is no place at all for me to hide.

CONVALESCENCE IN SUMMER 1949

I want no willow cabin at your gate,
Let me recall my soul which you have housed.
I'll not play David to your Saul, nor wait
With laurel wreath and rue while you, be-Mused,
Stretch ears to hear my scratching at your door,
Your hungry daemon fattening on my need.
Cured now of you, what matters is the core
Of me grafted to you for which I bleed.

THE GROCERY BOUQUET

Dear you and I are two who this year blessed
The spring's untenderness, the absence of
That time's intolerable tinder, the chime
Of iridescent wind, and birdsoft air.
No sweetness stabbed except the fact of you
Or I could not have borne being just a
Short walk and a lifetime away from you.
Though we endured the smell of hyacinth
And lilac grocery-bought we could not be
Apart now, love, had we passed these growing.
And though kind june begins without a rose,
I need november afternoons. I dread
The summer nights the raw remembering.

THIS NEIGHBORHOOD

"Now I am on the wing."

I have migrated to another place.
This neighborhood is not familiar. I
Walk safely down these streets without the face
That can be recognized, without the sly
And swaggering pretense of kindred heart
With which I wooed so desperately the bold
And myriad tenants of my life. Apart
At last and yet a part afire a-cold
Unfeathered but impassioned in the bone
Like dying Ivan I am on the wing
Articulate alight aloud alone.
Plucked clean and raw the skeleton will sing.

INCANTATE THE COCKATRICE

Cadenced in chromatic space
in a prismed carapace
Blown to blue Venetian bliss,
chant canticles to Nemesis.
Sing paeans to the precipice
of crescendoing embrace
to diminish the abyss.
Love, loud love is peril's grace.

SPENDTHRIFT

Coruscating in her bones —
Once she shone with precious stones.
Gone the coral parasol
Whose the moonstone buckled shoes?
Gone the rose embroidered hose
Gown and stole and camisole.

Vanity cross-gartered goes
Even in embroidered hose.
Watch the traitor turn his coat
With her jewels at his throat.
Undisguised the Pharisee
Smirks in her soul's panoply.

AUTUMN: EARLY MORNING

motionless morning
no quiver or tremor
in the meadows or
among trees flaring
in the fall of the year
I listen but cannot hear
a single bird anywhere
only the trilling whirr
of nameless insects shearing
the stillness the mist clears
blueness is there
every color shouts
as the sun comes out
and several birds are beginning
to sing

TWO SAPPHICS

Are you mine my love? Have I lost you to her?
Tell me. I am cold and afraid and I must
Know for I grow old and am lonely. Please SPEAK.
Hold me in your arms as you tell me and be brave.

How and when, why, where brute winds rose, waves rearing
Toppled, I know not. We had map and compass.
But . . . our ship foundered and when Helmsman reached
    shore
I, adrift, called back to our ship's SOUND: please LISTEN.

FRIGHT AMONG THE RUNES

Love, flute my veins
and float my bones
and freight my loins
to fruit our vines
but though you may be fraught with means,
my sweet love, never flout my lines.

CONVERSATION AT MIDNIGHT
WITH OSCAR WILLIAMS

You said the world has no identity
outside of each single human entity.
I said, wanting to keep the conversation light,
"The island oak that falls and none hears smite?"
Then you, not bothering to say "Of course,"
pursued your theme with measured gentle force.
"World evil's a reflection of your own,"
you said, "yours, his, hers, mine, and each alone."
I smiled, wooing the dialectic terror.
But later, goose-fleshed, stared into my mirror.

FEMININE ENDING OR,
ABANDONED, SHE DIED

The lark did all louden
The bees all were laden
All darkness was hidden
Bereavement no pardon
All sorrow forbidden
This May she'd been bidden
The morrow she'd wed on
The day that should sudden-
ly mistress this maiden
Nought wistful should sadden.
That lad she'd had pride in
did cruelly ride on
(a cad all unchidden)
with blooming bride on
the pillion beside in
gay ribbons to gladden
the frills she had tied on
the day that she died on.

BALLADE

Que fit Villon à la requête de sa mère,
pour prier Notre Dame

Lady of Heaven, Queen of nature,
Empress of every hellish district,
Receive me, your humble Christian creature
Of no worth, and in no way select,
That begs admission to your elect.
Your blessings, my Lady and Mistress,
Outweigh my sins and my distress,
Without your grace no soul could fly
To paradise, say I, no jesting songstress.
In this faith I will to live and die.

Tell your Son that I am His, His kin,
Plead that my sins by Him absolvèd be:
May I be shrived as was the Magdelene,
Reprieved as was the clerk Theophilus He
Pardoned and you forgave so mercifully
Despite his promise to the Anti-Christ.
Protect me from a sin so vast,
Virgin bearing the sacrament (by
And through Whom we worship) yet forever chaste.
In this faith I will to live and die.

I, a little woman poor and old
Who knows nothing, not one word have I read,
See in my parish church a gilt-gold
Paradise of harps and lutes, and see the dead,
Who die damned, boil in hell. Though dread
I feel from the one sight, the other quickens me.
Grant me that joyfulness, high Deity
To whom sinners must always return and reply.

138

In this faith I will to live and die.

Virgin, exalted Princess, you did bear
In your purity, Jesus, Whose empire
Lasts endlessly. Assuming mortal frailty, our
Lord left heaven to succour us by
Offering to death His body young and dear.
Noble thus was our great Lord, and thus Him I revere.
In this faith I will to live and die.

—*Francois Villon*

BALLADE

L'epitaphe Villon

You who outlive us, you, our mortal brothers,
Do not harden your quick hearts to
Us, for if you pity us poor others,
God will the sooner have mercy on you.
You see us hanging here, a wretched few;
As to our flesh which we have too
Much cherished, it is long since a putrid stew;
And we, the bones, are cindered and dissolved.
Let no one jeer the evil that we knew
But pray God that we all may be absolved.

Do not, because we name you brothers,
Disdain us, although we were killed, it is true,
In all justice. You know some men are wise and others
Foolish, that all men are not equally endowed. Then rue
This, but intercede for us who died, we do
Beseech you, with the Virgin's Son; sue
That the fount of His Grace which we did wantonly eschew
Still flow for us, that we from hellish blasts may yet be saved.
We are dead. Let no soul torture or beshrew
Us, but pray God that we all may be absolved.

The rain has drenched and scoured us, brothers,
We are dried black by the sun; a crew
Of crows and magpies have devoured our eyes; others,
Feathered and hungry, plucked us where beard and eyebrow
    grew.
Never at peace, we are forever helplessly askew
Here where our bones clattered as the winds blew.
Unendingly jostled and gyved are we who,
Pocked by the pecks of birds, are more revolved

By holes than is a thimble. Never join us, but in lieu
Pray God that all of us may be absolved.

Prince Jesus, Who is Lord of me and you,
Protect us from infernal sovereignty, do
Not allow that we with Lucifer become involved.
Mankind, be kind, mockery is not our due.
Pray God that all of us may be absolved.

—*Francois Villon*

FOLKWAYS

Was Galahad hired,
    Artemis laid?
Was Hercules tired,
    Ajax afraid?

The Argo was scuttled
    And Jason fleeced?
Ulysses a cuckhold,
    Aeneas beached?

O totem O Wildwood
O Autumn of Childhood
No heroes? No glories?
O Eros. O Mores.

" . . . NOR GOOD RED HERRING"

Between the violet and the void
Twixt the Adonai and adenoid,
Between the flambeau or the boy-beau
The martyred Joan or Alcott's Jo
Elsinore or Elsie D.
Cordelia or Corday C.
Adam's Eve or Little Eva
The hair shirt or the gay deceiver
Pity the pubic paradox
Goneril or Goldilocks —
Children I'll take growing old
Though doused the torch and dyed the gold.

TRIOLET

The bad die old
Kept quick by sin.
The good are sooner cold
The bad die old.
Though they be good as gold
The good can't win.
The bad die old
Kept quick by sin.

OF CONSCIENCE

The man who, doing violence, is saved
And, crime confessed, is by his victim shrived,
Sees, though he turn his back upon the mirror,
The lonely eyes of friends reflect this terror.

OF MERCY

Let Esau not enriched by Jacob's bounty be
But hang in peace like Judas on a flowering tree
Let Cain go forth all vulnerable without the brand
Crucify Herod and let Brutus die by Caesar's hand.
Thus we with traitor thoughts implore betrayal
And seek the victim's peace as holy grail.

NURSERY RHYME NO. 1

Sing a song of slaughter
A pocketful of bombs
Four and twenty children
Baked in their homes

Their homes are charred to cinders
Burned children do not sing.
Was not that a dainty dish
To set before the King?

The King was over at the mint
Spending all the money
The Queen was at the White House
Serving gall and honey.

The Generals in the Pentagon
Are planning our defense.
The people in the ghettos
Need bread for food and rents.

NURSERY RHYME NO. 2

Little Jack Horner
sat in a puddle
eating his Christmas Spam
He pulled out a pin
and lobbed the thing in
and said What a good boy I am.

THE MAN OF FAITH

The man of faith has fled the cross
And guilt becomes his albatross.
The politician's pity spends
No coin of mercy on his friends.
Old men devise new ways to die,
Let Icarus engage the sky.
Abraham's sacrifice is made—
The ewe lamb by the ram betrayed.
Though fear of love turn blood to ice,
I too have heard the cock crow thrice.

THE DISENCHANTED

Around herself she wove a rainbow web
    To keep the people out
    That she alone the shout
Of spring could hear. This child by whole
By fierce and loving focus of her soul
On sound of growing, taste of wind, did ebb
And flow with every tide and turn of season
Outside her was the cold grey world of reason.

When she is grown I think that she may say
    I wonder if they tried
    To make me come inside
If they had called with love I might have heard
And learned to answer to the spoken word
Now I hear sound of spring no more than they
Because the world is still outside, and grey.

DAUGHTER

Although you know that I denied the sun to you
You look at me with crocus eyes, and when you
Speak to me your robin voice sounds unbetrayed
By this your raw unseasonable april.

I am not deceived, my girl, I knew your loss;
And know again the fresh fact of that early pain.
But my conscience, humble hostage to your innocence,
Can be reprieved intact by your compassion.

THAT COMMON MOTH

for Louise Talma

The Common Moth feeds on woolen cloths,
others on furs or on the leaves of plants.
Not possessing *A Child's Book of Moths*,
I looked up Moth in dictionaries:
an Oxford, a Classical and a Dictionary of The Holy Bible.
I searched for Moths because I had observed one
as a friend and I were coming in
last night. Louise stopped, hushed me, and pointed to
a little moth hanging in the middle
of the back of the black screen door and
I wondered how many times that door
had opened and banged shut with comings and
goings while the little moth clung there
without stirring one of his black broidered
wings or his palest cocoa-colored
body etched with cosmic care; a death's
head there upon his body's back, mouth
hole, nose-holes, and eye-holes each side
of his spine, topped by a black cap: his
tiny head. His miniscule antennae
were stretched flat, and near his filament
right arms was a flattened bouquet
of flowerlets: seed sized and white.
"Eggs," declared Louise. Of course! A clutch
of eggs which will become small shining
worms. That smooth worm, that larva
that metamorphoses to moth.

152

"THE WHOLE WORLD'S IN A
TERRIBLE STATE OF CHASSIS"

Joxer said and the Paycock said
"I'm puttin' on my moleskin trousers"

You burrow through dusty labyrinths of time
rooting around or under the obstructing stone
scrabbling for the buried bone of Fido (or an ancestor)
never surfacing to be fractured by light
stabbed by jade blades stoned by the wind's weight
drowned in the sweet violent smells of dung roses seawater
blasted by explosions of bird song and hilarious children.
Your humped wake heaves a braille warning on the unguarded
lawns and in the wild dazzling gardens overhead.
You dare not burst through the earth's skin you are lonely
not perceiving tear totem fist nor phallus of your own kin
neither where you exist nor where the loud light lives.

FIXING THE CLOCK

Night after wakeful night, Woman, nightmares are real,
but day through sleeping day, Lady, daydreams are not.
Slow ticks fast tocks new rooms more clocks until your cot
that "fine and private place" admits embrace. Not soon
but if the clocks tick long enough then seize or steal
a tithe of time while the wound clocks are running on, not
down. Take time and take it soon some summer afternoon
for time is sure to fix your clock and all too soon.
Right now it's cold and lonely on that cot.
Therefore embrace! Fix time! Just stop the clock.

ONE SUNDAY IN 1966

       Sunday again
Never a week without Sunday
       Sunday you depress me
Dahlberg called you a mortuary day
I try reading the Times
I turn on the radio for news
The astronauts are orbiting space
One of them has a cold in the head
(both of my thumbs are arthritic
       I am all thumbs)
I had a party in this flat last night
Friends, lovers and strangers

I lie on an untidy sofa
and look away from pleasure's melancholy litter
       This place is a mess
I hold Jim Wright's book with arthritic thumb
and two viable fingers. I put the poems down
beside an inscribed-to-me copy of something
somebody gave me last night. I roll up the sleeves
of a man's shirt somebody gave me sometime or other
       This place is a mess
I collect motley glasses and ceramic ashtrays, souvenirs
of foreign parts or thrown by friends on a potter's wheel
I dump the butts down the toilet and the spit-backs in the sink
A glass I overlooked stands on the mantle piece
among delicate possibly rare objects bought by A.T. and me
ten years or more ago in Greece or Tuscany, antiquity
dubious. I want to read Jim's poems. This place is still a mess
       I know my age on Sundays

I shall not wash a glass
open a window answer a letter
pay bills organize files
or telephone anybody who cares long distance.
Instead I will take Sloth's
arm and go to a cryable movie
come back to the unaired flat
pick up the glass left on the mantle
rinse it fill it with wine
white iced and Tuscan go to my files
find under A: A.T.
I.G. letters: I need the earliest, the
in-the-beginning ones—
Spring Tide: Tug of the sun Pull of the moon.
Even today in 1979 I know my age on Sundays.

Note: "A.T." is the poet and critic Allen Tate, to whom Isabella Gardner had been married.

FLY IN AMBER

Myth tells us amber is the concretion
of tears wept by Meleager's sisters
before and after Artemis changed them
into long winged birds with horned beaks while they
mourned at Meleager's funeral pyre;
scooping up the ashes of their brother
with fingers stiffening to claws they pressed
their brother's ashes to dwindling breasts
beginning to feather, their lengthening
arms raised lowered flapped. The stretched holes of their
mouths contracted squeezed in pushed out curved down
hardened to horn became beaks North or East
South or West wherever the mourning sisters
flew their tears dropped. Should a tear drop upon
a leaf or an insect, on a fly for instance
then that tear drop would lumpen into clear
amber and the fly remain visibly
intact until Armageddon because
a dropped tear congealed an ambience to amber.

EROS IN MAY AT MacDOWELL

Softly wanton the wind
troubles the pungent air
lifting the pine boughs
sifting the pine needles
stirring and shifting
the lilac leaves and
spreading the plangent scent
of lilac. Shafts of lilac
arousing opening thrusting
heedlessly.
Never was I taken so
rashly and remembering
I nearly die! Again.

THE FELLOWSHIP WITH ESSENCE: AN AFTERWORD

THE FELLOWSHIP WITH ESSENCE:
AN AFTERWORD

> *Love consists of this: that two solitudes protect*
> *and touch, and greet each other.*
> — Rainer Maria Rilke

In so far as I am aware, I have never belonged to any school or coterie of thought or attitude. I have no dialectical approach to poetry. Not being an intellectual, or even cerebral, I work through instinct and intuition, through (or with) whatever I have acquired via my senses, a kind of osmosis.

I don't believe the poet should write with a cudgel, a lance or a crystal ball. A poet is no wiser, nor more compassionate than anyone else; yet I feel that the poet is focused on a particularized participation in the most minute or enormous instants, as well as in incidents of hourly existence. The poet is also presumably gifted with the ability to integrate and synthesize, to make vivid, to heighten and illuminate that awareness. If the poet is ferociously honest, fiercely intent in the act of writing, a poem is made. It may not be a good poem, it may be a bad poem; but it will not be a nothing.

Whether my own or that of another poet, I consider each poem as a separate, particular and immediate end in itself; a totality. However, if one reads or hears twenty or thirty — or even five or ten — poems by the same poet, there should be a recognizable voice, an individuality of tone, cadence and style of action and reaction within the poem.

Certainly, there will be recurring clues to, often proofs of, that poet's feeling toward those who share the human condition, toward that poet's life-experience and toward the work itself. The necessary nakedness involved in the act of writing is frightening to the poet, and often to others, and it contributes to a loneliness which in turn is exacerbated by the exhausting struggle to maintain the essential focus at whatever cost. A series of poems, a body of poetry, however small, is a declaration, a proof of a living human creature.

Karl Shapiro, in *Beyond Criticism*, said it for me when he wrote: "Poetry is the personal particular human truth which cannot be ordered or reasoned or pre-conceived, it can only be lived in life and made in art." Shapiro went on to say, "the limited personal truth of poetry and art gives the only permanent evidence of human reality we have."

If there is a theme with which I am particularly concerned, it is the contemporary failure of love. I don't mean romantic love or sexual passion, but the love which is the specific and particular recognition of one human being by another—the response by eye and voice and touch of two solitudes. The democracy of universal vulnerability.

Isabella Gardner
Summer, 1979

ISABELLA GARDNER

Born in Newton, Massachusetts in 1915, Isabella Gardner was a great-niece of Isabella Stewart Gardner (who bequeathed a museum to the city of Boston) and a cousin of Robert Lowell. With characteristic self-deprecating humor, Isabella Gardner insisted that she had received a minimal formal education. In fact, she attended the Foxcroft School, the Leighton Rollins School of Acting, and the Embassy School of Acting in London. She was a professional actress for several years and served as associate editor of *Poetry* from 1952 to 1956. During her lifetime Isabella Gardner published four compact and distinguished books of poetry: *Birthdays from the Ocean* (1955), *The Looking Glass* (1961), *West of Childhood* (1965) and *That Was Then: New and Selected Poems* (1980), which was nominated for the American Book Award for Poetry. In 1981, shortly before her death, Isabella Gardner was selected as the first recipient of the New York State Walt Whitman Citation of Merit for Poetry.

BOA EDITIONS, LTD.
AMERICAN POETS CONTINUUM SERIES